Waterfowl Hunting

Sloan MacRae

PowerKiDS
press

New York

Published in 2011 by The Rosen Publishing Group, Inc.
29 East 21st Street, New York, NY 10010

First Edition

Editor: Amelie von Zumbusch
Book Design: Greg Tucker
Photo Researcher: Jessica Gerweck

Photo Credits: Cover, pp. 4, 5, 6, 7, 8, 9, 10, 11, 13, 17, 18, 19, 23, 24, 25, 26–27 Shutterstock.com; p. 7 © www.iStockphoto.com/Brent Paull; p. 14 © www.iStockphoto.com/Ryan Howe; p. 15 Dennis Hallinan/Getty Images; p. 16 © www.iStockphoto.com/Andrey Nekrasov; p. 20 © www.iStockphoto.com/Charles Brutlag; p. 21 (top) Robb Kendrick/Getty Images; p. 21 (bottom) S. Solum/PhotoLink/Getty Images; p. 22 Mike Brinson/Getty Images; p. 28 Southern Stock/Getty Images; p. 29 Sandra Mu/ Getty Images.

Library of Congress Cataloging-in-Publication Data

MacRae, Sloan.
  Waterfowl hunting / Sloan MacRae. — 1st ed.
      p. cm. — (Open season)
  Includes index.
  ISBN 978-1-4488-0708-6 (library binding) — ISBN 978-1-4488-1377-3 (pbk.) —
ISBN 978-1-4488-1378-0 (6-pack)
  1. Waterfowl shooting—Juvenile literature. I. Title.
  SK331.M33 2011
  799.2'44—dc22

                                    2010008349

Manufactured in the United States of America

CPSIA Compliance Information: Batch #WS10PK: For Further Information contact Rosen Publishing, New York, New York at 1-800-237-9932

Contents

Can you outsmart a duck? It sounds easy, but ducks and other waterfowl are craftier than you might think. The term "bird-brained" does not apply to them. Different animals are hunted in different ways. Some hunters sneak through the woods to find their prey. Others sit silently for hours and wait for the animal to appear. Hunting

Waterfowl hunters need to keep their ears and eyes open and pay close attention to their surroundings, as this hunter is doing.

This young hunter has shot a duck. Ducks are one of the most commonly hunted kinds of waterfowl.

for waterfowl, or waterfowling, is unlike any other form of hunting.

Waterfowlers obey different hunting laws. They use different tools and tricks. All good hunters use their brains, but successful waterfowlers have to be extra clever. If you want to shoot a duck, you have to learn how to think like a duck.

Duck, Duck, Goose

"Fowl" is just another word for "birds." It usually refers to birds that you can eat. Waterfowl are birds that can be found near water. Some of the most common types are ducks, such as mallards, redheads, and wood ducks. Geese are waterfowl and can be hunted as well. They look a bit like ducks, but they are much larger.

These geese are Canada geese. Canada geese are among the most commonly seen kinds of waterfowl in North America.

Male wood ducks, such as this bird, are known for their beautiful coloring. Unlike most North American ducks, wood ducks nest in trees.

You have probably seen ducks and geese in ponds or lakes. They often swim together in groups. Shooting them does not seem hard if they are just floating on the water. What is so hard about waterfowling then? Where is the challenge?

A swimming bird is basically helpless. This is where the phrase "sitting duck" comes from. Some states

This duck is a male northern pintail. In this picture, you can see the long feathers in the middle of the bird's tail. These give the duck its name.

do not allow you to shoot waterfowl that are sitting or swimming. Most waterfowlers frown on shooting at a sitting duck. It is not **sportsmanlike**. The challenge of waterfowling is to shoot the bird in the air. Years ago, some North American waterfowl were nearly hunted to **extinction**. We now have laws to protect them.

These ducks are harlequin ducks. Harlequin ducks are sea ducks. They live in the northern Atlantic Ocean and the northern Pacific Ocean.

Learn to recognize waterfowl before you go hunting. It is against the law to hunt some waterfowl, such as whooping cranes like the one shown here.

Hunting laws for most animals vary from state to state, but waterfowlers obey lots of federal laws. These are the law no matter which state you are in. Waterfowling laws protect the birds from being wiped out. They also make the sport more challenging.

Flying South

Most North American waterfowl fly south during the winter. They head to warmer climates in order to survive. These annual migrations affect the hunting seasons, which are usually in the fall and winter.

Snow geese spend the summer in northern Canada and migrate to the United States and Mexico for the winter.

Hunting Facts

You can use Web sites such as www.ducks.org and www.waterfowler.com to track migrating waterfowl.

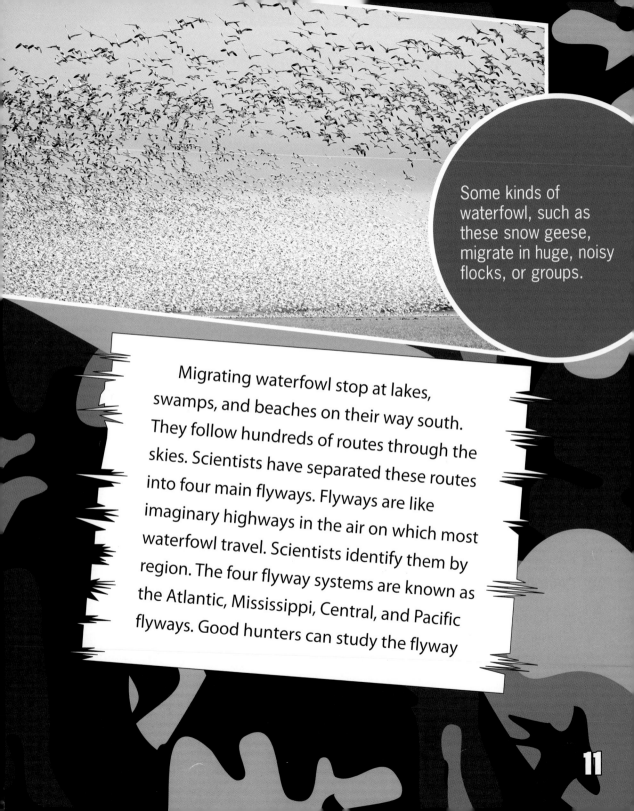

Some kinds of waterfowl, such as these snow geese, migrate in huge, noisy flocks, or groups.

Migrating waterfowl stop at lakes, swamps, and beaches on their way south. They follow hundreds of routes through the skies. Scientists have separated these routes into four main flyways. Flyways are like imaginary highways in the air on which most waterfowl travel. Scientists identify them by region. The four flyway systems are known as the Atlantic, Mississippi, Central, and Pacific flyways. Good hunters can study the flyway and migration patterns of their regions and learn the best times and locations to hunt.

It is important to make sure you know which waterfowl are in season before you go hunting. Check both the federal hunting laws and your state's hunting laws. It is illegal to shoot a bird that is not in season.

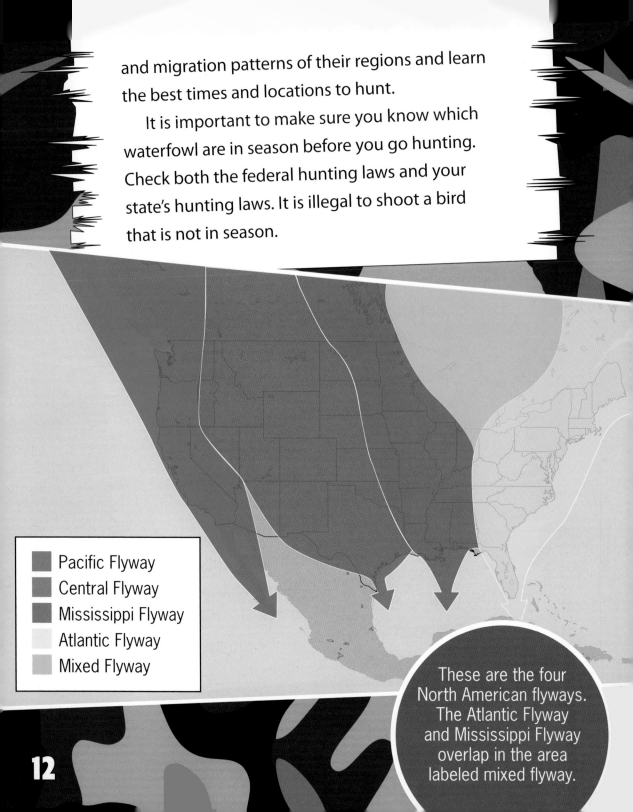

Pacific Flyway
Central Flyway
Mississippi Flyway
Atlantic Flyway
Mixed Flyway

These are the four North American flyways. The Atlantic Flyway and Mississippi Flyway overlap in the area labeled mixed flyway.

All hunters must carry hunting **licenses**. A hunting license proves that you are legally allowed to hunt a particular animal. To get a license, you must first pass a hunting safety course.

In addition to licenses, most waterfowlers are required to purchase **conservation** stamps. Hunters do not mind paying extra for these stamps because the

When hunters purchase conservation stamps, they are helping pay for the conservation of waterfowl habitats, such as the wetland seen here.

proceeds help protect **wetlands** and waterfowl **habitats**.

Conservation stamps are also called duck stamps. A duck stamp is like a second license. It looks like a postage stamp, but the picture is almost always of a duck. Do not put your duck stamp on an

This hunter's camouflage jacket and hat make it harder for waterfowl to see her as she hides in the tall wetland grasses.

Hunting Facts

Waterfowlers often stand in cold water. Waterproof waders will keep you dry. Waders are basically boots and overalls combined into one piece of clothing.

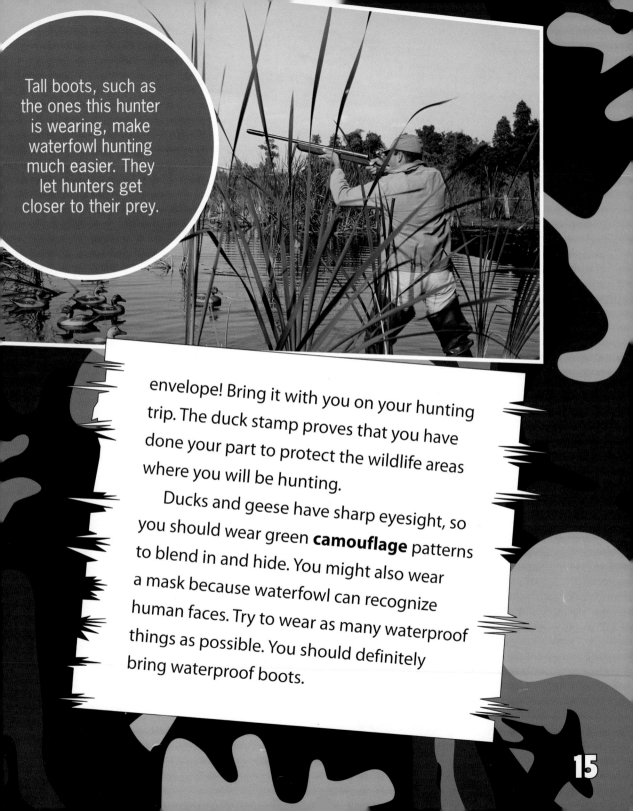

Tall boots, such as the ones this hunter is wearing, make waterfowl hunting much easier. They let hunters get closer to their prey.

envelope! Bring it with you on your hunting trip. The duck stamp proves that you have done your part to protect the wildlife areas where you will be hunting.

Ducks and geese have sharp eyesight, so you should wear green **camouflage** patterns to blend in and hide. You might also wear a mask because waterfowl can recognize human faces. Try to wear as many waterproof things as possible. You should definitely bring waterproof boots.

Shotguns and Trapshooting

The most important waterfowling tool is the shotgun. Shotguns do not shoot single bullets. They shoot shells that are packed with many small pellets, or shot. The shells explode and scatter the shot over a small area.

This hunter is aiming with her shotgun. Most waterfowl hunters use 12-gauge shotguns. However, 10-gauge shotguns and 20-gauge shotguns are also popular.

Hunting Facts

You have to be at least 12 years old to hunt. An adult must hunt with you.

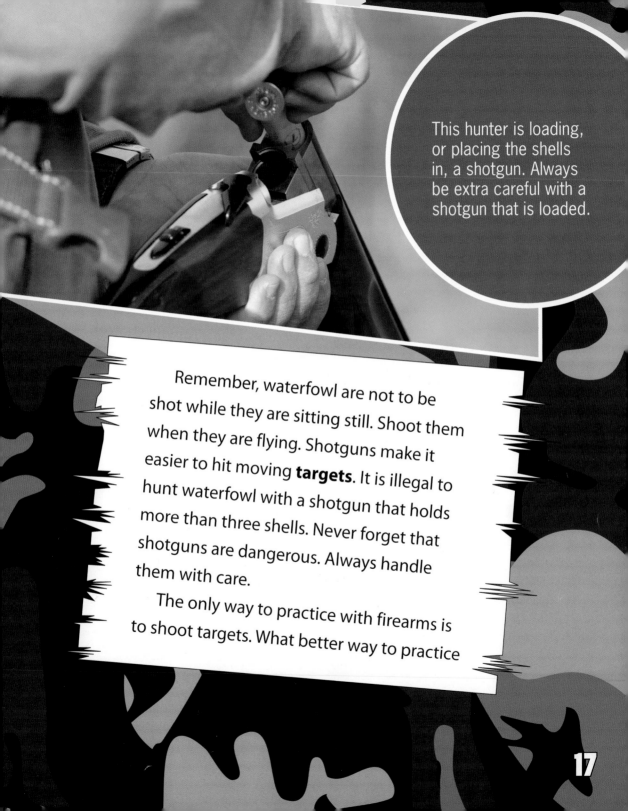

This hunter is loading, or placing the shells in, a shotgun. Always be extra careful with a shotgun that is loaded.

Remember, waterfowl are not to be shot while they are sitting still. Shoot them when they are flying. Shotguns make it easier to hit moving **targets**. It is illegal to hunt waterfowl with a shotgun that holds more than three shells. Never forget that shotguns are dangerous. Always handle them with care.

The only way to practice with firearms is to shoot targets. What better way to practice

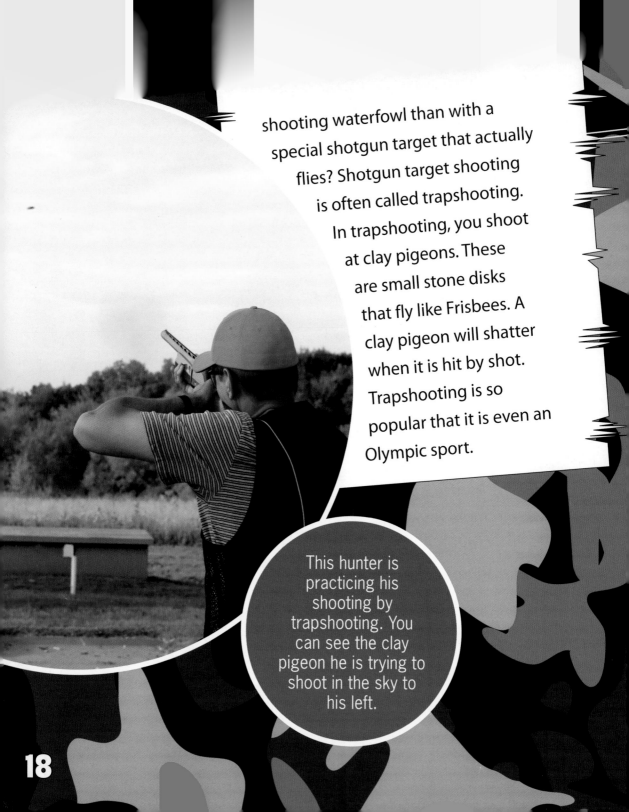

shooting waterfowl than with a special shotgun target that actually flies? Shotgun target shooting is often called trapshooting. In trapshooting, you shoot at clay pigeons. These are small stone disks that fly like Frisbees. A clay pigeon will shatter when it is hit by shot. Trapshooting is so popular that it is even an Olympic sport.

This hunter is practicing his shooting by trapshooting. You can see the clay pigeon he is trying to shoot in the sky to his left.

Be Smarter than the Duck

Hunting waterfowl is often like a game of hide-and-seek. The hunter wants to find the birds, but it is important to hide from them at the same time. Successful waterfowlers must be good at fooling their prey. Fortunately, there are several tools that can help.

This hunter is using real grass to make his camouflage jacket even harder to see. He is also setting up a hunting blind and using goose decoys.

One of the best waterfowling tools is the blind. A blind is a **screen** that conceals a hunter. Some blinds are tiny shacks. Others can fit over small boats. You can even create your own blind with branches and leaves. A blind is a form of camouflage.

This waterfowl blind was built in the middle of a lake. Waterfowl hunters must use a boat to reach it.

This hunter is setting out duck decoys. As hunters often do, he is using several decoys at the same time.

Waterfowlers also use decoys. Decoys are basically fake birds. They are often made from wood or plastic. Most of them can float. Some decoys even move like real birds. Good decoys will draw real waterfowl to them. Hunters used to tie ropes around live ducks to use them as decoys. This practice is now considered **cruel** and is no longer legal.

Some duck decoys, such as the one here, are beautifully made. In fact, some people collect duck decoys and show them off in their homes.

Another great waterfowling tool is the call. A call makes a noise that sounds like a particular waterfowl. Most calls look like kazoos. You blow into them to make the quacking sounds. Just like a decoy, a good call

This hunter is using a waterfowl call. There are many different kinds of calls.

can fool waterfowl into thinking that there are real birds nearby. Ducks and geese make noises to communicate. Different quacks mean different things. Waterfowlers can master this language and use many different calls to their advantage.

Dog Paddle

Many hunters get help from a dog. Some dog breeds, such as beagles and hounds, are good at finding game for the hunter to shoot. Dogs used for waterfowling are good at finding game after it has been shot.

Imagine you are in a thick swamp. You just shot a goose out of the sky. You have no idea where it landed. How will

Dogs are very helpful when hunting waterfowl. This dog is retrieving, or bringing back, a duck that its owner shot.

you ever find it? This is where a dog comes in.

Breeds like Labrador retrievers can locate the fallen birds and carry them back in their mouths to the hunter. It is like playing fetch, but the dog fetches birds instead of sticks.

This hunting dog is a Labrador retriever. These dogs were first bred by fishermen in Newfoundland, Canada.

Hunting Facts

There are several types of retrievers. The Labrador, golden, and Chesapeake Bay retrievers are some of the most popular pets in America.

Waterfowl hunting dogs, such as this golden retriever, are often good swimmers. They can easily retrieve birds that were shot over water.

Dogs that retrieve, or fetch, waterfowl are known as retrievers. These breeds even have webbed feet to help them swim! It helps if hunting dogs are well trained. They must be calm and quiet while on the hunt.

Waterfowlers might kill several birds in a single day, but they spend their lives saving hundreds of birds and other animals. Every time a hunter buys a duck stamp, that hunter protects waterfowl habitats. As scientists have pointed out, wetlands are valuable **ecosystems**. They are filled with many different kinds of insects, frogs, lizards, fish, birds, trees, and other plants.

Many hunters have joined the group Ducks Unlimited to preserve wetlands. Ducks Unlimited is the world's leader

Waterfowling organizations help preserve key waterfowl habitats, such as the pond where this mallard is swimming.

in the conservation of wetlands. The members of Ducks Unlimited work hard to protect waterfowl habitats from pollution and **development**.

Hunting Facts

You can join waterfowling organizations to learn the tricks of the trade. Some groups to check out are Delta Waterfowl and the North American Waterfowl Federation.

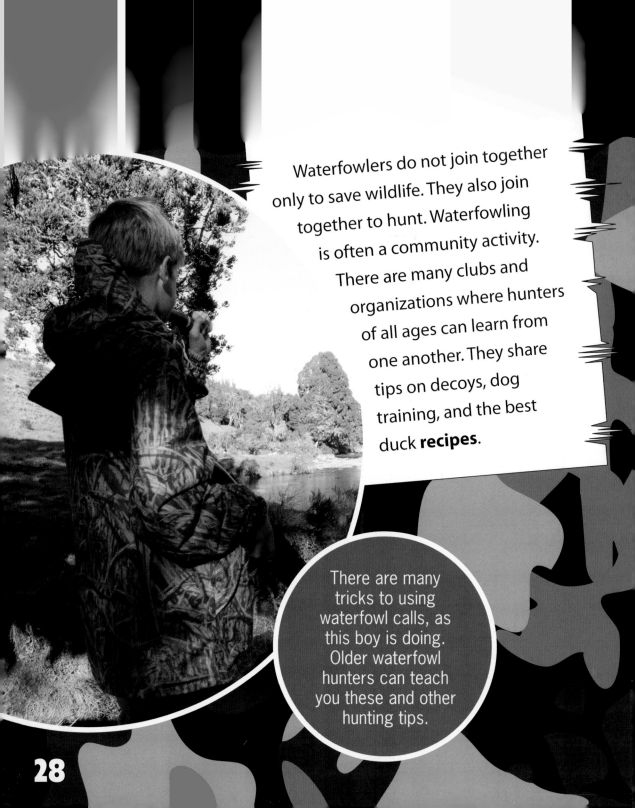

Waterfowlers do not join together only to save wildlife. They also join together to hunt. Waterfowling is often a community activity. There are many clubs and organizations where hunters of all ages can learn from one another. They share tips on decoys, dog training, and the best duck **recipes**.

There are many tricks to using waterfowl calls, as this boy is doing. Older waterfowl hunters can teach you these and other hunting tips.

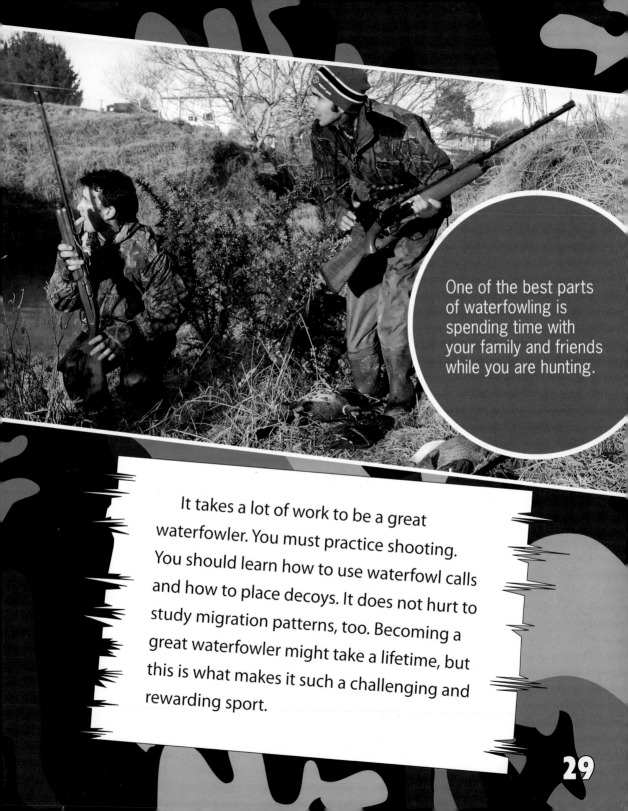

One of the best parts of waterfowling is spending time with your family and friends while you are hunting.

It takes a lot of work to be a great waterfowler. You must practice shooting. You should learn how to use waterfowl calls and how to place decoys. It does not hurt to study migration patterns, too. Becoming a great waterfowler might take a lifetime, but this is what makes it such a challenging and rewarding sport.

Happy Hunting

- Never hunt from a motorboat or sailboat. That is against the law.

- When you go waterfowling, bring waterproof clothing and boots. Being cold and wet will spoil your hunt.

- Make sure you know how to use duck and goose calls. Using them incorrectly will scare birds away.

- Remember not to shoot at ducks that are sitting on the water.

- Retriever puppies can learn a lot by hunting with older dogs. This is a great way to train them.

- Practice makes perfect. You can shoot trap by joining sporting and duck clubs.

- Be on the lookout for other waterfowl hunters. Unlike other kinds of hunters, they do not generally wear orange. This may make them harder to see.

- Never pull the trigger until you are absolutely sure of your target.

- Remember to clean and oil your shotgun after a hunt, especially if it gets wet.

- Have fun, and be careful!

Glossary

camouflage (KA-muh-flahj) Having to do with a color or a pattern that matches the surroundings and helps hide something.

conservation (kon-sur-VAY-shun) Protecting something from harm.

cruel (KROOL) Causing pain or suffering.

development (dih-VEH-lup-mint) Being built on.

ecosystems (EE-koh-sis-temz) Communities of living things and the surroundings in which they live.

extinction (ek-STINGK-shun) The state of no longer existing.

habitats (HA-buh-tats) The kinds of land where animals or plants naturally live.

licenses (LY-sun-sez) Official permissions to do things.

proceeds (PROH-seedz) The money made from selling something.

recipes (REH-suh-peez) Sets of directions for making things.

screen (SKREEN) A flat thing that hides or covers something.

sportsmanlike (SPORTS-mun-like) Fair.

targets (TAHR-gits) Things that are aimed at.

wetlands (WET-landz) Land with a lot of moisture in the soil.

Index

D
duck(s), 4–8, 14–15,
    21–22, 30

F
form, 5, 20

H
habitats, 14, 26–27
hunter(s), 4–5, 11,
    13, 19–21,
    23–24, 26, 28, 30

L
laws, 5, 8–9, 12
license(s), 13–14

M
migrations, 10

P
practice, 17, 21, 29–30
proceeds, 14

R
recipes, 28
redheads, 6

S
screen, 20

T
target(s), 17–18, 30

tool(s), 5, 16, 19–20,
    22
tricks, 5
types, 6

W
water, 6, 30
waterfowl, 4–8, 10–11,
    15, 17, 19, 21–22,
    25
waterfowler(s), 5, 8–9,
    13, 19, 21–22, 26,
    28–29
waterfowling, 5, 8, 23, 28,
    30
wetlands, 14, 26–27

Web Sites

Due to the changing nature of Internet links, PowerKids Press has
developed an online list of Web sites related to the subject of this book.
This site is updated regularly. Please use this link to access the list:
www.powerkidslinks.com/os/wh/